The
ROCK

George Goodman

ISBN 979-8-89243-476-8 (paperback)
ISBN 979-8-89243-477-5 (digital)

Copyright © 2024 by George Goodman

All rights reserved. No part of this publication may be reproduced, distributed, or transmitted in any form or by any means, including photocopying, recording, or other electronic or mechanical methods without the prior written permission of the publisher. For permission requests, solicit the publisher via the address below.

Christian Faith Publishing
832 Park Avenue
Meadville, PA 16335
www.christianfaithpublishing.com

Printed in the United States of America

Contents

Introduction v
1. The Encounter 1
2. The Rough Road Ahead 3
3. The Coming Horror 10
4. The Unbelievable Happens 19
5. A Whole New Life Begins 24
6. A Mighty Explosion of Love! 27

Introduction

This story is about a common man who earned a living as a fisherman. There was nothing unusual about this man until his life was changed by a new friend who offered to teach him certain things that would make his life better. This new friend of his was already gaining a reputation as an unusually knowledgeable and wise teacher about life.

Like most of us, this man—we will call Simon—wanted to build a better life for himself. He wanted to earn the love and respect of his family and friends and to be highly esteemed by his fellow laborers and the people he associated with day by day.

Simon would often speak his mind without thinking first. This would bring embarrassment and regret into his life experiences. He was always ready to try something new and different but often failed. This would make him feel worthless and miserable at times. Sometimes he, no doubt, felt all alone in this world as a complete failure that no one could love. But his friend would always be there for him and encourage him. Simon would never give up but kept trying. I think much of his persistent trying was because of his friend.

One day, something happened to Simon, that so drastically changed him that he became one of the most honored and respected men of his generation. What was it that could have made such a transformation in this man's life? We will see in the pages that follow.

1

The Encounter

Simon was a simple young man who was learning the trade of commercial fishing. He had hopes of earning himself and his family a comfortable living as he pursued this career. Everything seemed to be going good for him and his brother, Andrew, who worked with him as a fisherman. They had a boat and two close friends, James and John, who also had their own boat. They lived near a lake called Gennesaret, where they liked to fish.

There was a young rabbi from Nazareth, who was teaching in some of the synagogues there and in Capernaum. These two cities and Lake Gennesaret were in an area called Galilee. This rabbi quickly became well known and respected by many of the common people, who were amazed at the authority he taught with and the power he demonstrated. He spoke plainly and simply so he could be easily understood, and he also healed sick people and commanded bad spirits to leave them.

On the other hand, he was gaining hatred from the political and religious leaders because of the things he said and taught. They had recently attempted to throw him down a steep hill to his death, but he escaped from them.

Leaving Capernaum, he came to Lake Gennesaret, and the people who had heard of him and wanted to hear him began crowding around him. He saw that there were two boats there, and the fishermen were cleaning their nets, so he asked Simon if he could sit in his boat to speak to the people. Simon agreed, so he taught the people that morning for some time while Simon and Andrew and James and John cleaned their nets.

After he finished speaking, he asked Simon to launch out into the lake and let his nets down to see if he could catch some fish. Simon objected, saying, "We fished out there all night and caught nothing, and you want us to go back out there again. Besides, we just cleaned our nets, and we're tired. But if you insist, we'll go try it again."

When Simon and Andrew let the nets down, they were shocked! The nets were so full of fish they were on the verge of breaking! They even had to call James and John to help them get the fish into the boats. Then both boats were so full, they nearly sank. What a catch!

When this was all done, this young rabbi said if they would follow him, he would teach them how to not only catch fish but to catch people also. How could they not listen to and follow this man!? So they left everything behind and went with him. So began a whole new adventure and chapter in the lives of these four fishermen.

2

The Rough Road Ahead

Simon and his brother and two friends started off on this new adventure with great anticipation and excitement about their future. They would soon find, however, that they would face a lot of unpleasant situations and opposition that would accompany the wonderful times they would have while learning from this new friend of theirs.

When they left the lake and entered a certain city, they were met by a man who was full of leprosy. This man likely had drawn-up fingers, open sores that ran with puss and rotted tissue, a horrible sight to behold indeed. Not only that, but leprosy is a very contagious disease, and one should avoid getting near a person with leprosy. If you touched one such person, you would be classified as unclean and quarantined for seven days. Then the local priest would examine you, and if the leprosy appeared, you would be quarantined for the remainder of your life. You would usually be placed in a leper colony to ensure you would not infect any other people. The sight of this man must have aroused some fear of the disease in the rabbi's four friends. They shouldn't be anywhere near this poor man.

This man with leprosy had the unchecked audacity to ask the young rabbi if he would cure him of leprosy and even told him that he could if he really wanted to. This man's confident demand touched the rabbi's heart so much so that he was moved with compassion. He violated the safety and health regulations concerning leprosy and touched the man, saying, "I will. Be clean." To the great astonishment of the rabbi's friends, the man with the leprosy was healed of that great plague. The rabbi told him to keep quiet about it and to go offer the gift that the law of Moses required him to give to the priest for his cleansing.

This man went away healed and rejoicing, but he couldn't keep from telling everyone he saw what this rabbi did for him. This news of the leper's healing spread through the surrounding countryside until this young rabbi couldn't get any rest. They kept bringing to him all kinds of sick people for him to cure. He finally went into the wilderness with his four friends and prayed and rested. Simon and his friends could hardly believe what they were seeing.

As they were going to other towns where this young rabbi would teach and work miracles, they met a tax collector named Levi. This rabbi invited Levi to go with them. Levi had a dinner party prepared where he invited several of his friends. He likely wanted to tell them of his plans to go with this rabbi and his friends. The religious leaders became angry with him for eating with tax collectors and the likes. They considered the tax collectors to be evil people who served Rome and took money from the poor. He told them he didn't come to find and help the people who thought they were right and better than most, but he came to find and help the ones who knew they had problems and needed help.

Then on a Sabbath, he went into a synagogue to join with the worship. There was a man there whose hand was withered, so the leaders in the synagogue watched this rabbi to see if he would do any work on the Sabbath. If he did, they could accuse him of breaking the Sabbath. He knew what they were thinking, and he looked at them with disdain and anger. He asked them if it was lawful to do good on the Sabbath or to do evil. Then he asked the man with the withered hand to stand. Then he told him to stretch out his withered hand. The man did so, and his hand stretched out to be just like his good hand. He was miraculously healed.

Of course, this made the religious leaders even more angry with him because he not only broke the Sabbath but he also did a miracle that no one but God, or a great prophet, could ever do. He also silenced and embarrassed them in a horribly extreme manner.

THE ROCK

Simon and his friends were amazed at what he had done. They wondered what kind of man he was. No one could restore a man's withered or undergrown hand like that. And all he did was speak to him and tell him to stretch out his hand. He kept doing things that were impossible for any man. He was beyond incredible. This young rabbi went away from the crowds to find a place up on a mountain where he could get alone and pray. Then he spent all night praying.

By this time, he had a large company of people following him, so when he came down from the mountain, he chose twelve who had been following him closer than most. These twelve he designated as his representatives. He again taught the crowds of people and healed their sick.

After he finished teaching this crowd of people, he went to Capernaum where he could teach more people about God's love. Now, a certain Roman Centurion heard of his teaching and miraculous deeds. This centurion had a servant whom he loved like one of his own family. This servant was so sick that he was about to die. The centurion sent some Jewish elders to tell this rabbi about his servant. In his message, he first said he was not worthy that this rabbi should come under his roof but to speak the word only and his servant would be healed. He explained that he understood authority, saying he also was a man under authority, and he tells people to go or come, and they obey his orders. He understood this rabbi was under a higher authority and exercised that authority. The rabbi marveled at this man's faith, saying it was greater than any he had found in Israel. Just when he said this, the servant was healed.

In his travels with his friends and followers, he came to a city called Nain and encountered a widow whose only son had died. His body was being carried out in an open coffin. This young rabbi compassionately approached the widow and said, "Don't cry." Then he touched the coffin and said, "Young man, I say to you, arise." The man got up and was given to his mother. The people saw this and were amazed with wonder, saying, "God has visited his people and sent us a great prophet." So his fame was spread even more through all of Israel.

By this time, Simon and his friends were wondering what kind of man this rabbi was. He not only taught with an unusual authority but he also cleansed lepers by simply touching them; he healed all kinds of diseases with just his spoken word and even raised the dead by telling them to get up. There has never been a man like this!

But the political and religious leaders hated him and became more and more intent on having him killed or somehow getting rid of him. The things he said and did cause much people to follow him, and they were losing their control of the masses and some of their financial gain.

Soon after, he got in a ship with his friends and close followers and headed to the other side of a lake. He was tired, so he went to sleep. While they were crossing the lake, a great windstorm came up, and the waves began to fill the ship with water. They were terrified, thinking they were all going to die in the storm, so they woke up the rabbi and asked him why he didn't care that they were going to die. He got up and rebuked the wind and the waves. The wind stopped, and the waves calmed down. They were all astounded and wondered, "What kind of man is this?" He even commands the wind and waves, by simply saying, "Peace, be still."

When they got to the other side of the lake, a wildly crazy man came out of the graveyard. This man lived in the tombs and terrified passersby. He would cry and cut himself at night. They had tried to restrain him with chains and shackles, but he would manage to tear the chains apart and break the shackles. Furthermore, he didn't wear any clothes. When the rabbi saw him, he said, "Come out of him, you unclean spirit."

Then the man fell down and said, "What do I have to do with you, Jesus, you son of God most high? I beg you not to torment me."

Jesus asked him what his name was, and he replied, "Legion, because we are many. Please don't cast us into the deep but let us go into the swine."

Jesus let them go into the swine, and the whole herd ran down a steep place into the lake and drowned themselves.

The man who the rabbi cast the devils out of was suddenly sane, calm, and sound-minded. The gave him some clothes, and of course, he wanted to follow this rabbi. But the rabbi told him to stay and go tell the people around him what great thing God had done for him.

The keepers of the swine went and told the people in the city what had happened, so they came out to see it. Then they asked the rabbi to leave and not come back. They were afraid of him because he had demonstrated such great power and authority.

His followers were beyond themselves with astonishment at such wonderful things they had seen. But this was only the beginning. This rabbi would do things like this day in and day out like it was just the normal thing for him to do.

Now the religious leaders became more and more determined to destroy this rabbi because he was an increasing threat to their power over the people. They tried to dissuade the people from following him or even believing the things he taught. They even accused him of casting out devils by Beelzebub, the prince of devils. They likely reasoned that since the devils seemed to know him, he must have been a chief among them. So much more false accusations they used to try to get people to side with them and against this rabbi.

There soon came a time when this rabbi decided it was their turn do these wonders. He gave his twelve chosen followers authority over all devils and to heal the sick. Then he sent them out to tell the good news that the kingdom of God was near and to do the same miraculous things they had seen him do. They were now learning that they could do what this rabbi had shown them he could do.

A multitude of about five thousand men, plus the women and children with them, came to hear his teaching. When it grew late, his twelve followers asked him to send the crowd away so they could go get something to eat. The rabbi told them to give them something to eat, but they objected, saying, "Where can we get enough to feed this crowd of people? We only have five loaves and two fishes."

He said, "Make them sit down by fifties in a company." Then he blessed the food and broke it up to give to his followers who gave it to the people. Everyone ate to the full, and they took up twelve baskets of leftovers. "What kind of man can feed such a great multitude with a little lunch?" they wondered.

He asked his chosen twelve to get into a ship and go to the other side of the lake while he sent the crowd away. Having sent them away, he went up on a mountain to pray. When he was done praying, he walked out on the water to go to the other side of the lake. When his followers saw him, they thought they were seeing a ghost, but he said, "Be of good cheer, it is me."

Simon said, "Lord, if it is you, let me walk on the water to you." And he said, "Come." Simon got out of the boat and walked on the water toward the rabbi, but when he looked at the waves, he was afraid and started to sink, so he cried out, "Lord, save me." And the rabbi reached out his hand and lifted him up.

When they went into Caesarea Philippi, at the other side of the lake, he asked them who people said he was. They answered that some said he was John the Baptist, some Elijah, or one of the prophets. He asked, "Who do you say I am?"

Simon quickly answered, "You are the Christ, the Son of the Living God."

He said, "You're really blessed, for people did not show this to you, but my Father showed it to you. I call you Peter, and on this rock, I will build my church."

Peter must have felt really happy and proud of himself for this, but his pride would quickly vanish.

This rabbi, Jesus, began to tell them that he would be arrested, tried and crucified, and be raised again from the dead the third day after he was killed.

Simon Peter couldn't stand to hear that kind of talk, so he started to rebuke him, saying, "That be far from you, Lord. This can't happen to you!"

Jesus responded by saying, "Get behind me, Satan. You are an offence to me. You don't love the things of God, but the things of men." Peter's pride must have turned to shame and embarrassment.

Later on, he sent another seventy of his followers out to share the good news and to heal the sick and cast out devils. These seventy returned full of excitement and joy because of their experiences. They said, "Lord, even the devils are subject to us in your name!"

He answered, "I saw Satan fall from heaven like lightning. Look, I give you authority and power to walk on snakes and scorpions and over all the power of the devil. And nothing shall by any means hurt you. But in this, don't rejoice, but rejoice because your names are written in heaven."

The excitement grew and more people were coming to hear the teachings of this Jesus and his followers. Now his followers were learning to catch people, just like he said he would teach them to. Now instead of only one miracle worker who could heal the sick and cast out devils, there were more than eighty of them.

This caused the religious and political leaders of the day become so infuriated with hatred and anger that they would stop at nothing to get rid of this rabbi. They would spread the worst lies about him, trying to convince the people that he and his followers were possessed by and working for the devil. They labeled him a blasphemer and an insurrectionist so they could use their political influence with the Roman government to have him executed.

3

The Coming Horror

As time went by, the political and religious leaders became more and more determined to do away with this Jesus. He claimed to be God's Son, and his followers believed him.

On one occasion, he said to them, "Your father, Abraham rejoiced to see my day, and he saw it and was glad." Now Abraham is considered the father of the Jews because he trusted God, and the Jews are descendants of his grandson, Jacob.

The religious leaders became angry and said, "You're not even fifty years old, and you want us to believe you saw Abraham?"

Jesus answered, saying, "Before Abraham was I Am."

Now, the name God called himself when He sent Moses into Egypt to bring the Jews out of slavery was "I Am." So in saying "Before Abraham was I Am," he was claiming to be God. They considered this all the more reason to kill him.

A few days later, Jesus got word that a close friend of his, named Lazarus, was really sick. When he heard it, he said, "This sickness is not unto death, but for the glory of God, that the Son of God might be glorified thereby." Then he stayed where he was for two more days. Then he said, "Let' go into Judea again."

His disciples questioned his reasoning, saying, "The Jews recently tried to stone you, and you want to go back there?"

To this, he replied, "Aren't there twelve hours in a day? If anyone walks in the day, he doesn't stumble because he has the daylight, but if he walks in the night, he stumbles because there is no light in him. Our friend Lazarus sleeps, but I'm going to wake him up."

They responded, saying, "If he sleeps, he'll do well."

Then Jesus plainly said to them, "Lazarus is dead. And I'm glad for your sakes that I was not there to the intent that you may believe: nevertheless, let us go unto him."

Thomas, one of the twelve, said, "Let us also go, so we can die with him."

When they were coming into Bethany, where Lazarus had lived, his sister Martha met them and said, "Lord, if you had been here, my brother would not have died. But I know that even now, whatever you ask God, He will give it to you."

Jesus said, "Your brother shall rise again."

She said, "I know that he will rise again in the resurrection at the last day."

Jesus said, "I am the resurrection, and the life: he that believes in me, although he was dead, yet shall he live: and whoever lives and believes in me shall never die. Do you believe this?"

She answered, "Yes, Lord: I believe that you are the Christ, the Son of God who should come into the world." Then she went to get her sister Mary and tell her Jesus wanted to see her. Mary quickly got up and ran out to meet Jesus, and some of her friends followed her.

Jesus asked where they had laid him, and they showed him. It was a cave with a stone covering the entrance. Jesus told them to take the stone away, but Martha objected, saying, "By now he stinks. He's already been dead four days.

Jesus replied, "Didn't I tell you that if you would believe, you would see the glory of God?"

Then they took the stone away, and Jesus looked up and said, "Father, I thank you for hearing me. And I know that you always hear me, but I said it for these here, so they might believe that you sent me." Then he yelled, "Lazarus, come forth!" Then Lazarus came out of the cave wrapped in grave clothes with a napkin bound to his face.

Jesus said, "Loose him and let him go."

More multitudes of people believed on Jesus because of the raising of Lazarus from the dead, but the religious leaders were more determined to get rid of him, and some wanted to kill both Jesus and Lazarus to stop his followers from increasing in number and influence. They even had a conference to decide what to do about this Jesus because they were afraid that if Jesus continued doing these miracles, the Romans would take away their place and nation. At the conference, Caiaphas, who was the high priest, said, "You don't know anything, nor consider that it is expedient for us, that one man should die for the people, ant that the whole nation should not perish."

The feast of Passover, a week-long celebration of Israel's deliverance from four hundred years of slavery in Egypt, was fast approaching. Jews from all over were gathering to Jerusalem to make preparation for this feast.

Six days before Passover, Jesus went to Bethany to visit with Lazarus and his two sisters, Mary and Martha. Martha was serving while Jesus and Lazarus sat at the table talking. Then Mary took a bottle of very expensive spikenard ointment and anointed Jesus's feet with it and wiped them with her hair. The sweet aroma of the ointment filled the whole house. It was such a beautiful occasion, but Judas, one of Jesus' followers objected. He said, "Why wasn't this ointment sold for three hundred pence, the equivalent of about ten month's wages, and given to the poor. Why waste it?" He didn't say this because he cared for the poor but because he kept the money for Jesus and his disciples, and he was a thief.

Jesus said, "Leave her alone! She did this for my burial. You have the poor with you always, and you can give to them anytime you want, but you don't have me always."

Judas became enraged and went to see the religious leaders about how he could deliver Jesus into their hands. They agreed to give him thirty pieces of silver money for the task.

Jesus wanted to celebrate the Passover with his twelve chosen disciples, so he sent two of them ahead to secure an upstairs room and make the preparations for it.

When things were ready, Jesus and his twelve went into the upstairs room to celebrate the Passover feast on the first day of Passover. At the start of this feast, they would sing a hymn taken from the psalms, return thanks to God, and start. There would be a remembrance of Israel's deliverance from Egyptian slavery. This was then symbolized by dipping bitter herbs held by two pieces of unleavened bread into a mixture of raisons, dates, and such with vinegar to remind them of the bitterness of slavery. This then was followed by the meat prepared to remind them of the sacrificed lamb that was offered on the night the death angel passed over them and took the firstborn in Egypt.

When this meal was ended, Jesus took the bread, gave thanks, and gave it to the disciples, saying, "Take this and eat it. This is my body which is given for you: Do this in remembrance of me." Then he took the cup and said, "This is my blood which is shed for you." The disciples didn't understand that Jesus was indicating He was to be the sacrifice lamb of the new covenant God was making them and all who would believe. It would be about fifty days before they could understand this.

Then he told them that one of them would betray him. They questioned among themselves who it would be. Simon Peter said he would never betray him but would be imprisoned or even die for him.

Jesus told Simon that before the cock crew, he would deny that he knew him three times.

He started again to tell them that he would be arrested and put to death. They didn't want to hear anything of the sort, but he insisted that it was soon going to happen. He said also that three days after he died, he would be raised from the dead. They still didn't want to hear such talk, let alone believe it.

He led them out into the garden called Gethsemane, where he often went to be alone and to pray. He took his three closest friends a little farther than the other nine and asked them to wait there while he went to pray.

He prayed, saying, "Father, if it is possible, let this cup pass from me. Nevertheless, not my will, but yours be done." As he prayed, the agony of what he knew was coming was so severe that his sweat was like big drops of blood.

He went back to where his three friends were and said to Simon, "What? Couldn't you watch with me for one hour?" Simon must have felt like such a failure. How could he let Jesus down so badly?

Then he went away and prayed again, saying the same things. He prayed like this three times then returned to them, and said, "Sleep on now and take your rest. The son of man is betrayed into the hands of sinners. Get up now, let's go. He that betrays me is here."

No sooner had they gotten up from their sleep when Judas came with a mob of armed men and officers from the chief priests and religious leaders. Judas had given them a sign that the one he kissed would be Jesus, so he said, "Hail, Master." And kissed him.

They proceeded to take Jesus by force, but Simon, wanting to show his great devotion to Jesus, drew his sword and swung it at one of the men. This man was a servant of the high priest. His name was Malchus. Peter's aim must have been a little off because he only cut off his ear.

Instead of appreciating Simon's defense of Jesus, he told him to put up his sword. Then he picked up Malchus' ear, put it back on, and healed him. This must have made Peter feel like an unappreciated fool. He was only trying to defend Jesus. He must have felt unappreciated.

They forcefully arrested Jesus and took him to the home of Caiaphas, the high priest. Nine of Jesus' disciples scattered in fear of also being arrested, but Peter and John followed Jesus. John was known to the high priest, and he went in with Jesus, but peter stayed outside with the crowd that had gathered to see what was happening.

As Peter sat by the fire warming himself, a young lady saw him and said, "This man was also with Jesus."

Peter denied it, saying, "Woman, I don't know him!"

Then someone else saw him and said, "You are also one of them who was with him."

Peter denied him again, saying, "Man, I am not!"

Then a servant of the high priest, who was also a relative of Malchus, whose ear Peter cut off, saw him and said, "You are one of them. I saw you in the garden."

Then Peter started to curse and swear that he didn't know him.

THE ROCK

Then the rooster crowed, and Jesus looked at Peter. Peter remembered that Jesus had said he would deny him three times before the cock would crow, and he ran off and cried his eyes out. Peter failed again. He couldn't keep his promise to Jesus, his best friend, companion, and teacher. He felt so worthless. His life had no more purpose if Jesus was gone.

While Peter was watching from the outside, they blindfolded Jesus, spit in his face, slapped him hard in the face, and said, "Prophesy! Who hit you?" They mocked him horribly as they tortured him.

Caiaphas, the high priest, asked him if he was the messiah, the Son of God. Jesus replied, "I am: and you shall see the son of man sitting on the right hand of power, and coming in the clouds of heaven."

Caiaphas tore his clothes in disgust and said, "We don't need any more witnesses. You heard his blasphemy. What do you think?" And they all condemned him to death.

Because it was illegal for the Jews to execute anyone under Roman rule, they took Jesus to Pilate, a Roman ruler in Judea. They charged him with insurrection and accused him of stirring up the people, saying there was another king of Israel. They accused him of inciting rebellion against Rome.

Pilate interrogated him and found nothing to substantiate the charges. He was astonished that Jesus did not answer him about these accusations. Pilate wanted to release him, but the Jewish religious leaders insisted he be crucified.

It was customary to release one prisoner at the Passover, so Pilate, wanting to release Jesus, said he would chasten him and then release him. Then he had him severely whipped with a whip that was designed to rip the skin out when it was used, known as a cat of nine tails. Then the soldiers made a crown of thorns, shoved it into the top of his head, beat him severely, mocked him, and put a purple robe on him. He presented him to them, saying, "Behold your king."

The religious and political leaders of the Jews had so influenced the crowd that they cried out, "Away with him! Crucify him! We have no king but Caesar!"

Knowing they had brought Jesus to trial because of their own envy and lust for power, Pilate thought he could influence them to release Jesus by making them choose between him and a really evil insurrectionist and murderer.

He asked them if he should release Barabbas, who was a known murderer and insurrectionist, or Jesus, in whom he found no fault at all. The crowd, in moblike fashion, demanded he have Jesus crucified and release Barabbas.

Pilate didn't want to have a violent mob protesting his decision as a governor to release Jesus against the will of the people. That may have cost him, not only his position but also a possible banishment or imprisonment. At the least his competence to execute his office would be called in question by Rome. So he released Barabbas and delivered Jesus to the executioners.

The soldiers led Jesus to a hill called the place of a skull, where they crucified him and two thieves, one on each side of him. Pilate but a sign above his head which read, "King of the Jews." While this was being accomplished, at nine o'clock in the morning, the Jewish priests were offering the morning sacrifice of a lamb in accordance with the law of Moses.

The two thieves spoke harshly to him in a demeaning and evil manner, saying things like, "If you're the Son of God, come down from that cross" and "You saved others. Why can't you save yourself?"

Then one of them had a change of heart, saying, "Don't you fear God, seeing we are in the same condemnation as he is? And we deserve it, but this man has done nothing wrong!"

Then he said to Jesus, "Lord, remember me when you come into your kingdom."

Then Jesus replied, "Truly, I tell you, you shall be with me in Paradise today."

The leaders of the people who demanded that Jesus be crucified stood by, watching the crucifixion and taunting Jesus as they mocked him. They said things like He's calling for Elijah, let's see if Elijah will come to his rescue! When he said he was thirsty, they offered him vinegar. They kept verbally abusing him for about three hours.

THE ROCK

Then at about noonday, it got really dark, and the ground shook and cracked open, as the Earth quaked. This continued for about another three hours until three o'clock in the afternoon. The heavy curtain in the temple, which was made of blue, purple, and fine twined linen and embroidered with pure gold ripped apart from the top to the bottom. This curtain, called the veil, separated the holy place in the temple from the most holy place in the temple, where only the high priest could go once a year after offering a blood sacrifice.

At that time, Jesus cried with a loud voice, "My God, my God, why have you forsaken me?" Then he said, "It is finished." And died.

The day before the Sabbath was beginning at about six o'clock in the evening, and that particular Sabbath was more important than other Sabbaths because it was during Passover week. Because of this, the Jews asked Pilate to have the legs of the crucified persons broken so they would die quickly. You see, they could push themselves up with their feet and legs to prevent suffocation if their legs weren't broken. When the soldiers arrived to break the legs, they found that Jesus was already dead, so they did not break his legs, but one of them pierced his side with a spear. So none of his bones were broken.

There was a very wealthy man named Joseph who was a secret disciple of Jesus. He went and asked Pilate for the body of Jesus. Pilate gave him permission to take it, and another secret disciple, named Nicodemus, brought about a hundred pounds of a mixture of myrrh and aloes to prepare his body for burial. They wrapped him in linen cloth with the mixture and put him in a tomb in the nearby garden. This tomb was new, and no one had ever been put in it before. Then a stone was used to seal the entrance to the tomb.

When Judas, who had betrayed Jesus for thirty pieces of silver, saw that Jesus was condemned to death, he couldn't handle his overwhelming sense of guilt. He brought the silver back to the priests and tried to give it back, saying he had betrayed innocent blood. They told him that was his problem, and he should take care of it. They didn't care how he felt. He threw the silver at their feet and went and hanged himself.

Nine of the other eleven disciples had scattered in fear of their lives when Jesus was arrested. Peter and John had followed him to Caiaphas's house, but Peter fled when he was found out and had denied knowing Jesus. Now he was dead. All hope was gone. What was there to live for? The grief and mourning had now begun, and it was so hard. He had loved them more than any brother or sister could. He taught them about the kingdom of God. He sent them out in His name to heal sick people and even command devils to leave the people they oppressed. If the sorrow and grief weren't enough, they were now in fear for their own lives, knowing the soldiers could come at any moment to arrest or kill them for their association with this Jesus of Nazareth. They thought he was the messiah who would deliver Israel from Roman oppression, but now he was dead. What good was life now without Jesus?

The eleven disciples of Jesus and some friends and women retreated to an upstairs room, where they discussed the recent events ending with Jesus's death. They didn't know what would follow in the next few days and weeks but were in fear for their lives as the Roman soldiers might arrest or kill them any day.

4

The Unbelievable Happens

Early in the morning the first day of the week following the Passover Sabbath, some of the women took spices and went to the tomb to anoint Jesus's body. When they got there, the stone was already rolled away from the entrance of the tomb, so they went into it. When they did, they didn't find the body but saw what appeared to be two men dressed in shimmering clothes. These two asked them, "Why are you looking for the living among the dead? He is risen from the dead, just like he said he would." It was Mary Magdalene, Joanna, Mary the mother of James, and some others with them who came to find Jesus risen from the dead.

They went to tell the disciples and Peter what they had found and how the two men they saw, who were really angels, said Jesus had risen from the dead; but Mary Magdalene stayed behind in the garden by the tomb as she wept with grief and sorrow over Jesus's death. The two angels asked her why she was weeping. She said, "They have taken away my Lord, and I don't know where they laid him." Then she turned and saw a man, she thought was the gardener. He asked her why she was crying, and who she was looking for. She said, "If you've taken him away, tell me where he is, and I'll take him away."

He said to her, "Mary."

Upon hearing this, she turned and recognizing him, said, "Rabboni!?" (which means "master"). This title indicates he was a rabbi of rabbis, like a doctor of theology is today. Then Jesus said,

"Don't touch me yet because I have not ascended unto my father yet. Go to my brothers and tell them I ascend to my father and your father, to my God and your God."

After he saw Mary, Jesus ascended to his Father and returned to the Earth where he saw the other women. When they saw him, they held his feet and worshipped him then went to tell the other disciples he was risen and that they had seen him.

While the women went to tell the others, Jesus appeared to two disciples as they were going to Emmaus and talked with them about how the scriptures had foretold the death, burial, and resurrection of the messiah. Then he made himself known to them while breaking bread with them and vanished out of their sight.

When the women got back to the other disciples and told them Jesus was risen from the dead and they had seen and touched him, the disciples didn't believe them. They thought they were imagining things that just couldn't be real.

Peter and John ran to the tomb to see if what they heard was true, and they found the tomb empty, just as the women said. They found the grave clothes still in the tomb, and the cloth that was over his face folded by itself. Still they couldn't believe he was really risen from the dead but couldn't figure out what had happened. They hurried back to the others, who were in an upstairs room in fear of their lives for having been associated with Jesus, who was crucified for being a supposed threat to the religious and political leaders of Israel under Rome's rule.

As they discussed the recent events and how the one they thought would deliver them from Rome's oppression had been convicted by Pilate at an utter mockery of a trial and so cruelly tortured and crucified. The guilty shame and anguish Peter felt must have driven him to such despair that he despaired of life. How could he have promised to follow and defend Jesus even unto the death and then deny he ever even knew him!? All of them felt horrific shame and despair like Peter did because they all fled and left him, except John, whom the high priest knew.

While they were sharing their grief, anguish, and guilt, Jesus appeared in the room with them, greeted them with peace, and showed them his hands and feet that had been pierced through with nails. He told them he was sending them into the world just like his Father had sent him. Then he breathed on them and said, "Receive the Holy Ghost. Whoever's sins you remit, they are remitted, and whoever's sins you retain, they are retained." In this way, he was giving them full authority to speak, teach, and do the same things he spoke, taught, and did. When they acted in His name, he would ensure they got the same results he would have gotten. Then he asked for some food, and they gave him some fish and honeycomb, which he ate in front of them, showing himself to really have risen from the dead. A spirit does not have flesh and bones like he did.

Over the next forty days, Jesus taught his disciples from the Hebrew scriptures how that all the prophecies about his coming and his death and resurrection were fulfilled in him. He taught them that they would do the same works he had done and would be persecuted like he was but to rejoice in their sufferings because their eternal rewards would be far greater than any suffering in this life.

One day, Peter and several of the other disciples decided to go fishing. They went out in a boat and fished all night but caught nothing. In the morning, someone stood on the shore and asked if they had caught any fish. They answered no, and he said, "Cast the net on the right side of the ship, and you'll find."

They did as he had asked and caught one hundred and fifty fish that were so heavy they almost broke their nets.

Peter immediately shouted out, "It's the Lord." This was just like it was when he first met Jesus. They cast the net out like he said and caught so many fish they almost sunk both their boats. They were overwhelmed with joy to see Jesus again that morning. And not only did he see them, he also cooked breakfast for them.

After they ate, Jesus asked Peter, "Do you love me?"

Peter answered, "Yes, Lord, you know I love you."

Jesus answered, "Feed my lambs." And asked him again, "Do you love me?"

Peter said, "Yes, Lord, you know I love you."

Jesus answered, "Feed my sheep." And asked him again, "Do you love me?"

By this time, Peter was getting a little upset that Jesus kept asking if he loved him and replied, "Lord, you know everything. You know that I love you!"

Jesus said, "Feed my sheep. Truly I tell you, when you were young, you dressed yourself and went wherever you wanted to. But when you're old, someone else will stretch out your hands, dress you, and take you where you don't want to go." Jesus said this, signifying how Peter would die and glorify God even in his death. Then Jesus said, "Follow me."

Just before Jesus ascended back to his Father, he gave his disciples and friends some final instructions. He told them to wait in Jerusalem until the promise he had given them from his Father would come to them. This was the promise that the Holy Spirit would come and live in them, just as they had heard him pray, saying, "The glory which you gave me, I have given them, that they may be one, just like we are one. I in them and you in me, that they may be made complete in one; and that the world may know that you have sent me and loved them just like you have loved me."

He said that after they received the promise of the Father, they were to go into all the world and proclaim the good news of how God sent his only Son into the world to die in our place as a substitutional sacrifice to pay the death penalty for the sins of each person who would ever be born. And to teach them that believing on Jesus Christ and following him would bring them forgiveness of all their sins and bring them into a father-to-child relationship with God, who had created them. That relationship had been broken when the first man, Adam, had chosen to believe God's enemy, Satan, and rebelled against God. Because Adam was the father of all humankind, that choice to serve Satan resulted in the whole human race being enslaved to Satan and his evil nature. Jesus was the only man born without Adam's fallen nature, and he was free from sin. So he became the only perfect, sinless sacrifice for us to put sin away and give us God's holy and righteous nature in place of the depraved nature we inherited from Adam.

Jesus said these signs would follow those who believe and share this good news. In his name, they would cast out devils, they would lay hands on the sick, they would recover, and they would experience protection from poisonings and serpent bites.

The disciples and friends of Jesus were overwhelmed with excitement over all the things Jesus had said to them about their future. They were suddenly astonished as Jesus ascended out of their midst into the sky above them. As they gazed up, watching him, two angels appeared like men in shining white clothes standing beside them. These asked them why they were gazing up into the sky and said, "This same Jesus which is taken up from you will come again in the same way as you have seen him go up into heaven."

After this, the disciples and their friends gathered together in a large upstairs room in Jerusalem, where Peter, James, John, Andrew, Phillip, Thomas, Bartholomew, Mathew, James, Simon, Alphaeus, Simon, and Judas lived. There they continued to share their excitement about the recent events and the promise Jesus had made them. They spoke much about his death, burial, and resurrection, and how it fulfilled so many prophecies from the Jewish Tanakh. They enjoyed times of worshipping the God of Abraham, of prayer, and of sharing each one's experiences with Jesus. They did this for about seven to ten days, then everything in their lives dramatically changed. They would never be the same again.

5

A Whole New Life Begins

Now it was the Jewish Festival of Pentecost, a celebration of the giving of the Torah (the Law) from God to the Israelite nation, and a harvest celebration in which the first fruits of the harvest were brought to the temple as a sacrifice of thanksgiving unto God. This festival was first instituted fifty days after the Passover when God delivered the Israelites from slavery in Egypt. At that Passover, each family was to sacrifice a spotless lamb, paint the doorposts with the blood of the lamb, roast it with fire, eat it with unleavened bread and bitter herbs while dressed and ready to go on a journey. When the death angel passed through Egypt, the firstborn in all of Egypt would die, but if the house had the lamb's blood on the doorposts, no one in that house would die. Early the next morning, they left Egypt, only to be apparently trapped between the Red Sea and Pharaoh's pursuing army. But their God separated them from Pharaoh's army with a pillar of fire and parted the Red Sea so they could cross it on dry land. When Pharaoh's army pursued them into the Red Sea, God brought the waters back together and drowned the army. After four hundred years of slavery in Egypt, God brought them out with a mighty hand of deliverance.

Some fifty days after this, they were at the foot of Mt. Sinai, where God met with Moses, their leader. God called Moses up on the mountain, which seemed to be burning with a hot fire and covered with black smoke. There, God spoke to the Israelites from the mountain and gave them the Ten Commandments, which he also wrote on stone tablets and gave them to Moses. This, then, was the first Pentecost, when the law of God was given to people.

Pentecost was also the celebration of the great harvest they would enjoy in the promised land of Israel, which God said was flowing with milk and honey. This was the land God had promised Abraham he would give to his descendants. Because this was a special harvest celebration, Israelites from all the countries around would bring offerings of the first fruits to Jerusalem to offer them to God at the temple as a thanksgiving offering. So Jerusalem was filled with people who spoke several different languages, who came to offer gifts of thanksgiving in expectation of a great forthcoming harvest, blessed by God.

At this feast of Pentecost, there were about one hundred twenty men women and children in this upstairs room having a prayer meeting and worshipping God. Suddenly, it sounded like a strong wind rushed into the room and what looked like divided tongues of fire appeared on the heads of all of them, and they were all filled with the Holy Spirit. Then they started praising God and talking of His wonderful works in languages they didn't know. Some of the bystanders heard them and accused them of being drunk. Others questioned how this could be that these were all Galileans, and they were speaking in the languages of the Meads, Persians, Elamites, and several other languages. They were praising God for His wonderful works in all these different languages. These were not well-educated people, but common people who couldn't have learned so many different languages.

This was the fulfilling of the feast of Pentecost, as it was prophesied some 660 years earlier by Jeremiah, the prophet who said, "Behold the days come, says the Lord, that I will make a new covenant with the house of Israel, and the house of Judah. Not like the covenant I made with them when I brought them out of Egypt, which covenant they broke, even though I was like a husband to them. But this is the covenant I will make with the house of Israel, after those days, says the Lord. I will put my laws in their inward parts and write them on their hearts, and I will be their God and they shall be my people. They won't need to teach each other to know me, because they shall all know me, from the least to the greatest. For I will forgive their iniquity, and I will remember their sin no more."

Because Jesus had become sin and died as the perfect sacrifice lamb of God on the cross of Calvary, their sins had been put away, the penalty having been put away by the shed blood of Jesus. This made the way that God, the Holy Spirit, could now live in his people and write his laws upon their hearts.

When Jesus was buried, he was the seed of this new kind of person God was creating in His people. As He had said in John chapter 12 verse 24, "Unless a grain of wheat falls into the ground and dies, it lives alone. But if it dies, it brings forth much fruit." Jesus, in His death, burial, and resurrection was that seed that would bring forth much fruit. In Revelation chapter 1, verse 5, Jesus is referred to as the firstborn of the dead. In His resurrection, Jesus was the first fruit of this new creation.

When the promise of the Father came into that upstairs room and the Holy Spirit came into those worshippers, the first fruit offering was completed. What a marvelous day. These all had entered into the new covenant God had made in Christ Jesus. Now they had been united with Christ in His death and resurrection. This meant they were new creatures in Christ.

A whole new life was beginning, wherein people could know God and fellowship with him as their personal Father.

6

A Mighty Explosion of Love!

While the onlookers were wondering what was happening and trying to make some kind of sense of it, Peter, who had previously felt like a cowardly failure at following Jesus, stood up with the other disciples and addressed the crowd with great boldness. He said, "You men of Judah, and all you that dwell at Jerusalem, be this known to you, and listen to my words! These men are not drunk as you think, seeing it is only nine o'clock in the morning. But this is that which was spoken by the prophet Joel, 'And it shall come to pass in the last days, says God, I will pour out of my spirit upon all flesh: and your sons and your daughters shall prophesy, and your young men shall see visions, and your old men shall dream dreams: and on my servants, and on my handmaidens I will pour out in those days of my Spirit; and they shall prophesy. And I will show wonders in heaven above and signs in the earth beneath—blood, and fire, and vapor of smoke. The sun shall be turned into darkness, and the moon into blood, before that great and notable day of the Lord come. And it shall come to pass that whoever shall call on the name of the Lord shall be saved.' You men of Israel, hear these words; Jesus of Nazareth, a man approved of God among you by miracles, wonders and signs, which God did by him in the midst of you, as you yourselves know; Him being delivered by the determinate counsel and foreknowledge of God, you have taken, and by wicked hands have crucified and slain: Whom God has raised up, having loosed the pains of death: because it was not possible that it should hold him. For David spoke concerning him, 'I foresaw the Lord always before my face, for he is on my right and, that I should not be moved: Therefore, did my heart rejoice, and my tongue was glad; moreover, also my flesh shall rest in hope: because you will not leave my soul in hell, neither will you allow your holy one to see corruption. You have made known to me the ways of life; you will make me full of joy with your countenance.'

"Men and brothers, let me freely speak to you about the patriarch David, that he is both dead and buried, and his grave is with us today. Therefore, being a prophet, and knowing that God had sworn an oath to him, that of the fruit of his loins, according to the flesh, he would raise up Christ to sit on his throne; he, seeing this before spoke of the resurrection of Christ, that his soul was not left in hell, neither did is flesh see corruption. This Jesus, God has raised up, of which we are all witnesses. Therefore, being exalted by the right hand of God, and having received of the Father the promise of the Holy Spirit, he has shed forth this which you now see and hear. For David is not ascended into the heavens: but he says, himself, 'The Lord said unto my Lord, you sit on my right hand till I make your enemies your footstool.' Therefore, let all the house of Israel know assuredly, that God has made that same Jesus, whom you crucified, both Lord and Christ."

When the crowd heard these bold words from Peter, they were pricked in their hearts and said, "Men and brothers, what should we do?"

Then Peter said, "Repent and be baptized in the name of Jesus for the remission of sins, and you will receive the gift of the Holy Spirit. For the promise is unto you and to your children and to all that are afar off, even as many as the Lord our God shall call."

Peter continued to testify and exhort about how Jesus died, was buried, and rose again to save us from our sins and enslavement to sin.

Many of those who heard Peter believed on Jesus and were baptized. About three thousand people were saved and added to the church that day, seeing and hearing the wonderful things God had done through the name of Jesus. This was only the beginning of what was to happen.

Peter and John went to the temple one day at the time of prayer, which was three o'clock in the afternoon. There they encountered a crippled beggar who was over forty years old and regularly begged at the entrance to the temple grounds. This beggar asked them for some money, but they didn't have any. Peter looked at him and said, "Look at us. I don't have any money, but I'll give you what I do have. Then he said, "In the name of Jesus Christ of Nazareth, rise up and walk." And he took him by the right hand and helped him get up on his feet. All of a sudden, his feet and ankle bones became strong, and he went into the temple with Peter and John, and he was walking, jumping for joy, and praising God.

When the onlookers saw him walking and jumping, they recognized that he was the same crippled man who had been begging there every day for years. They wondered how this could be possible, and when they saw he was with Peter and John, they ran up to them, seeing they had performed this great wonder that made this cripple walk again. How could they have given this man, who was born crippled the power to walk and even jump?

When Peter saw this, he spoke up boldly to explain this to the people. He said, "You people of Israel, why do you marvel at this? Why do you look so intently on us, as though by our own power or holiness we had made this man to walk? The God of Abraham, and of Isaac, and of Jacob, the God of our fathers, has glorified his son, Jesus, whom you delivered up, and denied him in the presence of Pilate, when he was determined to let him go. But you denied the holy one and the just and desired a murderer to be granted unto you and killed the prince of life, whom God as raised from the dead, whereof we are witnesses. And his name, through faith in his name has made this man strong, whom you see and know—yes, the faith which is by him has given him his complete soundness in the presence of you all. Now I know that you did it through ignorance, which also your rulers did. But those things which God had before shown by the mouth of all his prophets, that Christ should suffer, he has so fulfilled. Therefore, repent and be converted that your sins may be blotted out when the refreshing times shall come from the presence of the Lord, and he shall send Jesus Christ, which before was preached unto you: whom the heavens must receive until the times of restitution of all things, which God has spoken by the mouth of all his prophets since the world began. For Moses truly said unto the fathers, 'A prophet shall the Lord your God raise up unto you of your brethren, like unto me; him shall you hear in everything he shall say unto you. And it shall come to pass that every person that will not hear that prophet shall be destroyed from among the people.' Yes, and all the prophets from Samuel and those that follow after, as many as have spoken have likewise foretold of these days. You are the children of the prophets and of the covenant which God made with our fathers, saying unto Abraham, 'And in your seed shall all the peoples of the earth be blessed.' Unto you first, God having raised up his son, Jesus, sent him to bless you in turning every one of you away from his iniquities."

While Peter was still speaking, and John was also teaching the people about the death, burial, and resurrection of Jesus, the priests, temple captain, and the Sadducees came to confront them. The Sadducees were a religious sect of the Jews who did not believe there ever was or ever would be any resurrection of the dead. These were grieved and angry because Peter and John taught the people that Jesus was resurrected from the dead, and that through faith in the name of Jesus, they, too, would be resurrected and live forever with Jesus. They took them and put them in hold overnight since it was getting late. However, while they were being arrested, many of the people who heard them believed and committed their lives to this risen Christ Jesus, who had healed this crippled man and given such boldness of speech and fearlessness to two common, uneducated fishermen who had been with Jesus. The number of men who believed was about five thousand, besides women and children. This new kind of life was exploding in Israel and changing people at a rapid pace!

In the morning, Annas, the high priest, Caiaphas, John, Alexander, and many of Annas's kinfolk were gathered together at Jerusalem. These were many of the same people who orchestrated the mockery of a trial where Jesus was condemned to death. These same people had excited so much fear in Peter that he denied three times ever knowing Jesus. They brought Peter and John out to be interrogated by these men, who asked them, "By what power or by what name have you done this?"

Then Peter, filled with the Holy Spirit, answered with great boldness, "You rulers of the people and elders of Israel, if we are this day examined of the good deed done to the impotent man, by what means he is made whole? Be it known unto you all and to all the people of Israel that by the name of Jesus Christ of Nazareth, whom you crucified, whom God raised from the dead, even by him does this man stand before you whole. This is the stone that was cast aside by you builders, which has become the head of the corner. Neither is there salvation in any other, for there is none other name under heaven given among men, whereby we must be saved."

When they saw the boldness of Peter and John, they marveled at it, knowing they were simple, uneducated fishermen. It was obvious that they had been greatly affected by the time they had spent with Jesus. And seeing the man that was healed standing before them, they could say nothing against it. So they set them aside and held a conference to determine what they should do.

They didn't know what to do. A great miracle of healing was done by these two, and everybody in Jerusalem knew it! After all, this man was born crippled; and now he was walking, jumping, and dancing with joy. To make it even more exciting and influential with the public, this man was over forty years old! How could they stop this teaching about the death, burial, and resurrection of Jesus of Nazareth from spreading through all of Israel? If what they were preaching about Jesus was true, then he really is the messiah, and there is no more need for the priesthood, the sacrifices, or any of their services. Their control of the people and their livelihood was at stake. They decided their best option was to threaten them with severe consequences if they continued to preach or teach in the name of Jesus.

They called them back and threatened them, forbidding them to speak at all in the name of Jesus. This would not be allowed in Israel anymore.

Then Peter and John answered them, "Is it right or wrong in the sight of God to listen to you more than to God? You judge. Because we can only speak about the things we have seen and heard."

Since they could not punish them for healing the lame man because all the people glorified God for what was done, they further threatened them and let them go.

Upon being released, they went to the local group of followers of Jesus and told them what had transpired. When they heard about them having been arrested and threatened, they didn't express anger or resentment. They didn't talk about protesting or staging a demonstration against the Jewish leaders or the Roman government. Instead, they called a prayer meeting. They didn't complain to God about their persecution or the threats. They glorified God, who made the heavens and the earth. They quoted the Word of God in their prayers, as David said, "Why do the heathen rage, and the people imagine vain things?" Then they said in their prayers that the kings of the earth and the rulers gathered together against the Lord and his Christ. Truly, Herod, Pontius Pilate, the gentiles, and the people of Israel gathered against your holy child, Jesus, whom you anointed. They did what your hand and your counsel had already determined to be done when they had him crucified. And now, Lord, look at their threatenings and grant your servants boldness to speak your word by stretching forth your hand to heal and that mighty signs and wonders may be done by the name of your holy child, Jesus."

When they finished praying, the place where they stood shook, and they were all filled with the Holy Spirit and preached God's Word with great boldness.

More people joined with them and followed the teaching of Jesus and his disciples. There was a great explosion of wonders and healings, insomuch that people started bringing their sick friends and relatives to them in the hopes that if even just the shadow of Peter passed over them they would be healed.

This angered the high priest and all that were with him, mostly Sadducees, who did not believe there was a resurrection. They had them arrested and put in prison.

That night, God sent his angels to them. The angels opened the prison doors, brought them out of the prison, and told them to go stand in the temple and speak to the people about the wonderful words of this new life in Christ Jesus.

Early next morning, they sent some officers to the prison to bring them back for questioning. When the officers returned, they reported that the prison was safely locked and the keepers were standing guard, as they should. Everything was in order, but the prisoners they were calling for were gone.

Then someone came in and told them he had seen those same men they had put in prison out in the temple. And they were teaching the people in the name of Jesus, the very thing they had been imprisoned for. So the priests, and those that were with them, went to the temple and brought them back. They did this as peacefully as they possibly could because they didn't want to cause an uproar. They knew that many of the people believed their teachings and were uniting with them in their doctrine.

They again reminded them that they have strictly forbidden them to teach or preach in the name of Jesus. To this, Peter and the others answered, "We should obey God rather than man. The God of our fathers has raised up this Jesus, whom you killed and hanged on a tree. God has exalted him at his right hand to be a prince and a savior, to give repentance and forgiveness of sins to Israel. And we are his witnesses of these things, and so is the Holy Spirit, whom God has given to them that obey him."

This angered them so much, they wanted to kill them for disregarding their directives. Then Gamaliel, a Pharisee who was very well known and respected among them and among all of Israel, as a teacher of the Torah, spoke up. He said, "If this movement is of man, it will pass in time, so there is no urgency to fight it, but if it is of God, beware that you don't fight against God." They listened to Gamaliel's advice. So they beat them and further forbid them to preach or teach in the name of Jesus.

Peter and others like him continued to preach and teach in the name of Jesus as time went on. Countless miracles of healing, casting out of devils, and even raising the dead were done by them in the name of Jesus. The persecution from the Jewish temple worship leaders, the Roman government and other religious groups would not only continue but greatly increase. These men endured these persecutions without bitterness or resentment. Rather, they counted it a privilege to suffer for Jesus, the only Son of God, who had suffered such a horrific death to save them from sin and give them eternal life. They never credited themselves with any of the miracles and wonders done by their hands, but gave all the glory to God, who had given them the authority to use the name of Jesus, and He would do the miraculous works for them. Just as Jesus gave all the glory for his deeds to the Father, so these gave all the glory to Jesus.

Peter so loved the Lord, who called him out of his humble fishing career to follow him, that he spent his life serving him and telling others of the love of Jesus. He not only told of God's love, but he demonstrated it with miracles of healing, deliverance, blessings of every kind, and even the raising of the dead. He continued to boldly proclaim the Gospel of Jesus Christ in the face of persecutions, stonings, imprisonment, and finally giving up his life. Peter was crucified upside down for saying he was not worthy of being crucified like Jesus was.

Peter is a great example of the new life in Christ Jesus. Such a marvelous transformation in his life. Yet for all this, Peter enjoyed nothing that we can't experience today if we just commit our all to Him.

About the Author

George Goodman, the fourth son of a Church of God, Cleveland, Tennessee, preacher was born in Casper, Wyoming, in the spring of 1951. The first eight years of his life were spent in Wyoming, Colorado, California, and Texas. His parents, Clarke and Doris Goodman, moved reasonably often due to opportunities for pastoral ministry and the ability to find gainful employment as a union painter.

While living in Texas, in 1958, Clarke became acquainted with T. L. Osborne, world-renowned evangelist, who had a tremendous influence on his family. Clarke would show Osborne's documiracle films in various churches spread the gospel and raise funds for the Osborne ministry.

At the age of twenty-one, George committed his life to Jesus. This was the glorious start of his new and wonderful life in Christ Jesus.

George graduated from Christ for The Nations Institute in Dallas, Texas, in 1976. He has been involved in teaching, preaching, deliverance ministry, and evangelism. He is an ordained minister in the Church of God of Cleveland, Tennessee.